jB
K58643H14

MAR 09

CH

Martin Luther King Jr.:
Civil Rights Leader

written by M. C. Hall   illustrated by Marty Martinez

Content Consultant:
Richard Jensen, PhD
Author, Scholar, and Historian

Beginner Biographies

magic wagon

visit us at www.abdopublishing.com

Published by Magic Wagon, a division of the ABDO Publishing Group, 8000 West 78th Street, Edina, Minnesota 55439. Copyright © 2009 by Abdo Consulting Group, Inc. International copyrights reserved in all countries. All rights reserved. No part of this book may be reproduced in any form without written permission from the publisher.

Looking Glass Library™ is a trademark and logo of Magic Wagon.

Printed in the United States.

Text by M.C. Hall
Illustrations by Marty Martinez
Edited by Nadia Higgins
Interior layout and design by Emily Love
Cover design by Emily Love

Library of Congress Cataloging-in-Publication Data

Hall, Margaret, 1947-
  Martin Luther King, Jr. : civil rights leader / by M.C. Hall ; illustrated by Marty Martinez.
      p. cm. — (Beginner biographies)
  Includes index.
  ISBN 978-1-60270-251-6
  1. King, Martin Luther, Jr., 1929-1968—Juvenile literature. 2. African Americans—Biography—Juvenile literature. 3. Civil rights workers—United States—Biography—Juvenile literature. 4. Baptists—United States—Clergy—Biography—Juvenile literature. 5. African Americans—Civil rights—History—20th century—Juvenile literature. I. Martinez, Marty, ill. II. Title.
  E185.97.K5H255 2009
  323.092—dc22
  [B]
                                        2008002892

Table of Contents

A Matter of Color

Martin Luther King Jr. was born in Atlanta, Georgia, on January 15, 1929. Martin's father was a minister at an African-American church. His mother had been a teacher.

Martin grew up listening to his father speak at church. He became a good speaker himself. He even won prizes for speeches he gave at school.

Martin was born in 1929.

5

In 1929, segregation was everywhere in the South. Segregation laws kept African Americans and whites apart. African-American children couldn't go to school with white children. African Americans and whites couldn't drink from the same drinking fountains. They couldn't eat at the same restaurants.

Martin's parents taught him that the color of a person's skin didn't matter. However, Martin knew it did matter to some people. When he was six, he became friends with a white boy. Then the boy's father said his son couldn't play with African-American children.

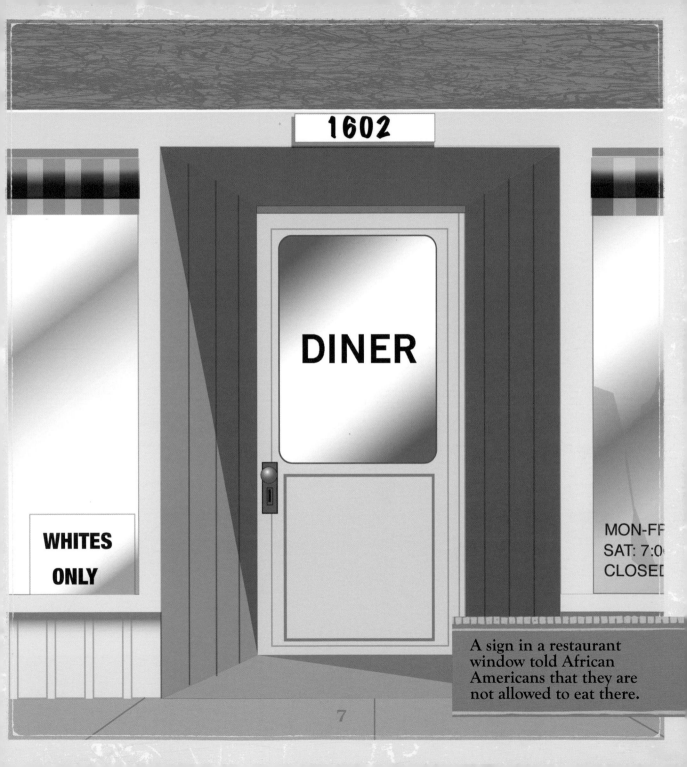

1602

DINER

WHITES ONLY

MON-FR
SAT: 7:0
CLOSED

A sign in a restaurant window told African Americans that they are not allowed to eat there.

When he was a teenager, Martin took a summer job on a farm in the North. He saw African Americans and whites working together. They went to the same churches. They shopped at the same stores. Martin wanted life to be like that in the South, too.

In the North, Martin sat next to a white woman at church.

Martin and Coretta Scott were married.

10

Years of Study

When he was 15, Martin started college at a school for African-American students. He thought about becoming a doctor or lawyer. Then he decided to be a minister, like his father. He wanted to help African Americans. He wanted segregation to end.

To become a minister, Martin Luther King Jr. needed more school. He went to another college where most of the students were white. King became a class leader, anyway.

While he was still in school, he met Coretta Scott. They got married in 1953.

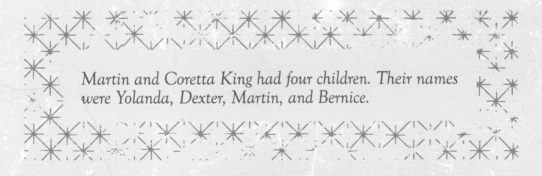

Martin and Coretta King had four children. Their names were Yolanda, Dexter, Martin, and Bernice.

In jail, a police officer took Rosa Parks's fingerprints.

A Move to Montgomery

After college, King decided to become a minister in Montgomery, Alabama.

In Montgomery, the bus company had unfair rules. African-American passengers had to ride in the back of the bus. If a bus was full, they had to give their seats to white passengers.

One afternoon, a woman named Rosa Parks got on the bus. She was tired after a long day of work. She wouldn't give her seat to a white passenger. The bus driver called the police. They took Rosa Parks to jail.

Protesting for Change

African Americans were angry. King led a boycott against the bus company. He asked all African Americans to stay off the buses until the rules changed.

The boycott made some whites angry. They sent letters saying they would hurt King and his family. Someone even threw a bomb at his house. However, King refused to fight back.

King didn't believe in violence. He said, "We must meet hate with love."

King led many civil rights protests.

15

It took more than a year for the boycott to work. The U.S. Supreme Court finally said the bus company's rules were unfair. The company could not make African Americans move to the back of the bus. It could not make them give their seats to whites.

King was happy that his peaceful protest had worked. He wanted to work harder against segregation. He led protests against other unfair laws. He told his people not to fight if they were arrested.

After the boycott, African Americans were free to sit anywhere on the bus.

Police sometimes sprayed King and his fellow protesters with fire hoses.

King and his followers had to be brave. People threw stones and dirt at them. The police sometimes sprayed them with fire hoses. Many of them were sent to jail. King ended up in jail, too.

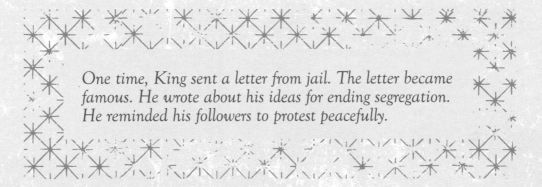

One time, King sent a letter from jail. The letter became famous. He wrote about his ideas for ending segregation. He reminded his followers to protest peacefully.

Protesters climb aboard a bus for a Freedom Ride.

FREEDOM NOW

FREEDOM'S WHEELS

FREEDOM'S WHEELS ARE ROLLING

LAW OF THE LAND IS OUR DEMAND

Marching for Freedom

Many people listened to King. African Americans and whites rode together in buses across the country. They called their trips Freedom Rides. Freedom riders led marches in the cities they traveled to. They carried signs that said segregation should end.

In August 1963, more than 200,000 marchers went to Washington, D.C. King made a speech there. He said, "I have a dream." His dream was that his children would not be judged by the color of their skin.

More and more people started to listen to King and other African-American leaders. In 1964, a new law passed. The Civil Rights Act said all people have the same rights. The color of a person's skin didn't matter.

King's work made him famous around the world. In 1964, he received the Nobel Peace Prize. This prize is one of the most respected awards in the world.

King gave his famous
"I have a dream" speech
in Washington, D.C.

23

King went to jail
for his beliefs.

24

King knew there was still a lot of work to do. Some states tried to make it hard for African Americans to vote. King led a protest and went to jail again. Some whites said they would kill him.

Even some African Americans were angry at King. They said peaceful protests weren't enough. They wanted to use violence to change things.

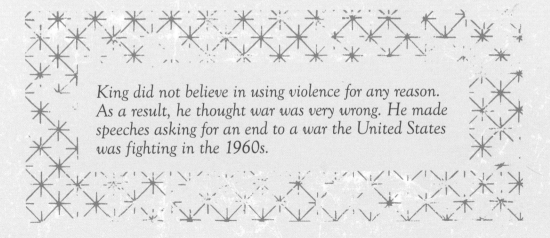

King did not believe in using violence for any reason. As a result, he thought war was very wrong. He made speeches asking for an end to a war the United States was fighting in the 1960s.

But King wouldn't give up his peaceful protests. He went to Memphis, Tennessee, to lead a march. This protest was to help workers who were being treated unfairly.

The evening of April 4, 1968, King was at his motel. He stood outside talking to friends. Then there was the sound of a gun. A white man named James Earl Ray shot and killed King.

More than 100,000 people went to King's funeral. They wanted to honor him for his bravery. They wanted to thank him for his work.

Honoring Martin Luther King Jr.

Now there is a special day for remembering and honoring King. Every year, we celebrate Martin Luther King Jr. Day on the third Monday of January.

Every year, people march in a parade to honor Martin Luther King Jr.

FUN FACTS

✦ The Montgomery bus boycott worked because most of the people who rode the buses were black. Without black riders, the bus company couldn't make money.

✦ At age 35, King was the youngest person ever to receive the Nobel Peace Prize. The prize came with more than $50,000. King did not keep any of the money for himself. He gave it away to help his cause.

✦ King gave a speech just before he died. He knew that there were many threats against his life, but he was not afraid to die. He said, "I'm so happy tonight. I'm not worried about anything. I'm not fearing any man."

TIMELINE

1929 Martin Luther King Jr. was born on January 15.

1953 King married Coretta Scott.

1955 Rosa Parks was arrested on a bus for not giving up her seat to a white passenger; King led a successful boycott against the bus company.

1963 King gave his "I have a dream" speech in Washington, D.C.

1964 The Civil Rights Act was passed.

1968 King was shot and killed on April 4.

1983 Martin Luther King Jr. Day became a national holiday.

GLOSSARY

boycott—to refuse to deal with a person, store, or organization until they agree to certain terms.

Civil Rights Act—an act passed in 1964 that made discrimination based on race, religion, or national origin unlawful.

minister—a person who leads church services.

protest—to speak or act against something.

segregation—the separation of an individual or a group from a larger group.

U.S. Supreme Court—the highest court in the United States. The Supreme Court makes decisions about laws and how they are followed.

violence—fighting to physically hurt people.

LEARN MORE

At the Library

King, Martin Luther Jr. *I Have a Dream*. New York: Scholastic, 2007.

Marzollo, Jean. *Happy Birthday, Martin Luther King Jr.* New York, Scholastic, 2006.

Sexton, Colleen A. *Let's Meet Martin Luther King Jr.* Philadelphia: Chelsea House, 2004.

On the Web

To learn more about Martin Luther King Jr., visit ABDO Publishing Company on the World Wide Web at **www.abdopublishing.com**. Web sites about King are featured on our Book Links page. These links are routinely monitored and updated to provide the most current information available.

INDEX